MW01610774

Cate Blanchett: Icon of Style and Success

The official tribute to the contemporary film muse and award-winning world star

Daniela Connor Grayson

Introduction

Cate Blanchett is not only one of the most internationally recognised and acclaimed actresses, she is a figure of rare versatility, elegance and talent who has left a profound mark on the world of film, theatre and popular culture. Her career is a journey that winds its way through dramatic and comic roles, historical characters and fictional figures, always boldly exploring the most complex nuances of being human. Blanchett is known for her ability to reinvent herself in every performance, demonstrating a dedication and commitment to her craft that transcends the simple act of acting. Every time she appears on screen, be it Hollywood blockbusters or independent productions, Cate brings with her a magnetic stage presence, capable of capturing the audience's attention and bringing her characters to life in an authentic and unforgettable way. Cate Blanchett's career has been built on a series of courageous and well-considered choices, which have enabled the actress to distinguish herself from the start as a major figure on the international film scene. Born and raised in Australia, she has managed in just a few years to move her career on a global scale, working with some of the greatest directors of our time and receiving numerous awards for her work. But what makes her career truly unique is her ability to combine mainstream success with a commitment to auteur cinema, a combination few actresses can boast of. Despite numerous awards and accolades, Blanchett has never been content to rest on her laurels. On the contrary, each new project has been an opportunity for her to challenge herself, explore new territory and hone her acting skills. Her tireless approach to acting, her passion for art and her willingness to always take on new challenges have made her one of the most respected and influential artists of her generation. Beyond the iconic roles she has played, Cate Blanchett has also made her mark in the world of theatre, dedicating herself to innovative productions and contributing to the artistic direction of the Sydney Theatre Company. Her commitment behind the scenes demonstrates how deep her passion for all forms of dramatic artistry runs and how strong her desire to contribute to the growth of theatre and film culture, not only in Australia but around the world. Blanchett's influence goes beyond her work on set: she is a leader in the gender equality movement in Hollywood and an advocate for environmental causes, making her an example not only of artistic talent, but also of civic and social engagement. This book is a tribute to the extraordinary career and personality of Cate Blanchett, one of the most emblematic and influential figures of our time. By exploring her life, her most iconic performances, her triumphs and her challenges, readers will have the opportunity to learn more about the artist and woman who has transformed every role into a work of art and continues to inspire millions of people around the world. Blanchett exemplifies artistic excellence, dedication and commitment, and this tribute seeks to capture the depth and complexity of her journey, which is not only a story of success, but also of growth, transformation and passion for art in all its forms.

-Arguments-

Chapter 1. The origins of a precocious talent

Cate Blanchett was born on 14 May 1969 in Ivanhoe, a suburb of Melbourne, Australia. Her family, consisting of a Texan father who worked as a merchant navy officer and an Australian mother who taught at a primary school, gave her an environment of great openness and intellectual curiosity. The sudden death of her father, when Cate was only ten years old, left an indelible mark on her life. This event not only made her more aware of the fragility of life, but also accentuated the bond with her mother and her two brothers. Growing up in an environment that encouraged artistic expression, she developed a strong interest in theatre and acting as a child, participating in school plays and demonstrating a natural talent early on. Despite her reserved nature, Cate has always shown a propensity for exploring characters, stepping into roles with a depth that hinted at her future potential. During her teenage years, she began to experiment with her interest in visual and performing arts in a more structured way. This came first through interaction with the world of film, of which she was an avid spectator, and then with theatre, which fascinated her for its immediacy and intensity. The influence of her family, who always supported her artistic inclinations, was crucial in giving her the confidence to follow her dream. After completing high school, she decided to enrol at the University of Melbourne, but finding no inspiration in business and fine arts studies, she soon dropped out. It was during this academic hiatus that Cate decided to go on an educational trip that would take her to Europe and, most importantly, Egypt, where she had one of the most life-changing experiences. During her stay in Cairo, she was invited by chance to participate as an extra in an Egyptian film, an experience that rekindled in her the desire to act and pushed her to take the path of film and theatre more seriously. Back in Australia, she decided to study acting more systematically and enrolled at the National Institute of Dramatic Art (NIDA), the country's most prestigious acting school. It was here that she began to hone her skills, learning acting techniques that led her to distinguish herself for her dedication and multifaceted talent. During these years, she starred in several major theatre productions and began to be noted both for her stage presence and her ability to play a wide range of characters. One of the first roles she played, and which had a major impact on her career, was that of Elektra in a production of the Greek tragedy of the same name. The success of this play cemented her reputation as an up-and-coming actress and opened the door to important collaborations, including some with the Sydney Theatre Company, which she would later lead with her husband Andrew Upton. These early years of her theatrical career were a crucial training ground for Cate: the theatre, with its need for constant presence and intensity, forged her as an actress, allowed her to explore the deeper nuances of characters and develop the refined technique she would later bring to the silver screen. Blanchett has always recognised how crucial the theatre played a role in her artistic training. Through her years of apprenticeship on Australian stages, she learnt not only how to play complex characters, but also how to handle the pressure and responsibility of big roles. This early phase of her life was marked by a sense of personal and professional growth, which saw her emerge with a clear vision of what she wanted to do as an actress. The influence of her family, always ready to support her, combined with the discipline and commitment she developed during her studies and early theatre experiences, created the basis for what would become one of the most extraordinary and respected careers in show business.

Chapter 2. The rise in Australian theatre

Cate Blanchett has always considered theatre the place to hone and test her talent, and it was here that she took her first significant steps. After completing her training at the National Institute of Dramatic Art (NIDA), one of the most prestigious institutions in the Australian theatrical world, the young Cate began acting in a series of productions that immediately brought her into the spotlight. Among her first major roles were performances in classics such as David Mamet's 'Oleanna' and Caryl Churchill's 'Top Girls', two plays that allowed her to showcase her extraordinary ability to play complex and nuanced characters. However, it was the role of Elektra, in the Greek tragedy of the same name, that gave her her first truly great recognition. The way in which she was able to embody the character's suffering and anger deeply impressed audiences and critics alike, demonstrating her talent for bringing dramatic roles of impressive psychological depth to life. This period of professional ascent brought her into contact with some of the most influential theatre directors on the Australian scene, key figures who would shape her path and contribute to the emergence of the refined and powerful acting technique that has always distinguished her.

One of these key encounters was with Neil Armfield, director and artistic director of Sydney's Belvoir

Theatre Company. Armfield was one of the first to recognise in Cate a special talent, capable of completely transforming herself into any character. Their partnership led to collaboration in several successful plays, including 'Hamlet', where Cate played Ophelia, and Anton Čechov's 'The Seagull', in which she played Nina. In these performances, Blanchett not only impressed with her stage presence, but also with her ability to make the characters incredibly real and human, a skill that would secure her the attention of international critics. Success in Australian theatre led her to become a leading figure in the Sydney Theatre Company (STC), one of the country's leading theatre companies. There she began working with a range of talented directors, contributing to productions ranging from classics to contemporary plays, always with an absolute dedication to perfecting her craft. Cate approached each role with a depth and awareness that went beyond mere interpretation: for her, each character was an opportunity to explore new aspects of the human condition, and the theatre was the perfect laboratory for doing so.

During this period, Cate developed an acting technique based on a rigorous control of her body and voice, elements that became the hallmark of her performance. Her ability to switch from intense dramatic roles to lighter ones with surprising ease demonstrated a versatility rare among actors of her generation. Each character seemed a reflection of a part of her artistic soul, and Blanchett never spared herself in searching for the emotional truth behind each performance. Her preparation for each role was meticulous: she spent weeks studying the text, worked closely with the directors to explore the deeper motivations of the characters, and often spent a great deal of time analysing the interactions between the different characters in the play. This level of commitment made her one of the most respected actresses in the Australian theatre world and laid the foundations for her future international career.

Success at the Sydney Theatre Company was only the beginning of a path that would see her evolve in extraordinary ways. Blanchett, along with her husband Andrew Upton, would later become co-artistic director of the company, bringing new life and innovation to productions and keeping theatre at the centre of Australian cultural life. During her leadership, Cate not only continued to perform in highly successful productions, but also turned her hand to directing, once again demonstrating her versatility. With Upton, she formed a creative team that managed to stage a series of innovative and courageous plays, always maintaining a high level of quality and artistic challenge. Although her name was beginning to be known internationally, especially thanks to her early film successes, Cate never abandoned the theatre. For her, the stage represented the place where the actor's true craft was put to the test, without filters, without editing, in a direct confrontation with the audience. This deep connection with Australian theatre has been, and continues to be, a constant in her career, even in her most successful moments on the big screen.

Cate Blanchett's rise in Australian theatre represented a period of intense personal and artistic growth, where she not only honed her technical skills, but also developed a clear vision of her identity as an actress. Her encounters with influential directors, the complex roles she played and her success in the Sydney Theatre Company prepared her for the success she would later achieve internationally. The theatre provided her with the foundation on which to build an extraordinary career based on a relentless pursuit of authenticity and truth in every performance. Blanchett has never been an actress who was content to be a star: her goal has always been to grow as an artist, to explore every angle of acting and to test herself in different contexts, and theatre has been the essential starting point for her to become the global icon she is today.

Chapter 3. The international film debut

Cate Blanchett's international film debut marks a crucial turning point in her career, catapulting her from Australian theatre to the global stage. Having built a solid reputation in the theatre world, it was only a matter of time before the cinema recognised her extraordinary talent. The first major role that brought her into the limelight was in the film 'Paradise Road' (1997), directed by Bruce Beresford, a choral production that told the story of women interned in a Japanese prison camp during World War II. In this film, Blanchett played a nurse, a secondary role, but her sincere and passionate performance did not go unnoticed. Although the film was not a huge commercial success, critics began to notice the young Australian actress for her ability to communicate emotional intensity with disarming simplicity. However, it was the 1998 film 'Elizabeth' that finally established her on the international scene. The role of Elizabeth I of England, the Virgin Queen, was a major test for Cate, and her performance earned her an Oscar nomination for Best Actress, as well as a shower of critical acclaim. Shekhar Kapur's direction highlighted her ability to dominate the screen with charisma and intensity. Blanchett's transformation of the shy and vulnerable young queen into a powerful and confident figure capable of ruling a nation was rendered with a psychological precision and emotional depth that surprised even the most discerning critics. The performance not only demonstrated her dramatic talent, but marked the beginning of a career that would see her tackle increasingly complex and challenging roles.

Critical reactions to 'Elizabeth' were enthusiastic. Blanchett was described as an actress capable of bringing a historical figure to life with a modernity and vulnerability that made her extraordinarily human, combining regal grace and inner strength. Her work was praised both for the depth with which she tackled the role and for her ability to embody such a complex character with apparent ease. The nominations and awards were not long in coming: in addition to an Oscar nomination, she won a BAFTA and a Golden Globe, unmistakable signs that a new star was shining in the Hollywood firmament. The film not only consolidated his reputation, but opened up a series of opportunities in top-level projects. Hollywood, always on the lookout for new talent, began wooing Cate Blanchett with roles in major production films. Her prowess did not go unnoticed even by fellow actors and directors, who immediately regarded her as a professional of the highest calibre, capable of combining rigorous theatrical discipline with the flexibility required by the cinema.

After 'Elizabeth', Blanchett received a series of offers that demonstrated her versatility and her desire not to be labelled into one genre. In 1999, she starred in 'The Talented Mr. Ripley' directed by Anthony Minghella, a psychological thriller in which she played Meredith Logue, a rich and naive heiress who unwittingly finds herself caught in the web of lies woven by the character of Tom Ripley, played by Matt Damon. Even in a secondary role, Cate managed to steal the show, confirming her ability to bring memorable characters to the screen and to make a difference even in a high-level ensemble cast. The film, a success with both critics and audiences, further helped cement her status as an actress capable of switching genres with ease.

But the real leap into Hollywood cinema came with her role in Peter Jackson's Lord of the Rings trilogy, where she played Galadriel, the majestic elven queen. The character, although not one of the main ones, had a significant impact on fans and audiences alike, thanks to her ethereal and charismatic performance. Her participation in one of the most ambitious film projects of all time marked the beginning of a new phase in her career, in which Blanchett proved to be at ease not only in historical or dramatic roles, but also in the world of fantasy and large commercial productions. The global success of the trilogy helped to further strengthen her presence in international cinema, paving the way for increasingly diverse roles. His ability to switch from intense dramatic roles to characters in large commercial franchises has been one of the keys to his long-term success.

With her international film debut, Cate Blanchett not only demonstrated her extraordinary talent, but inaugurated a career that would be studded with courageous choices and unforgettable performances. Her approach to film, rooted in her theatrical training, allowed her to bring to the big screen a level of authenticity and intensity that has always distinguished her. In every role, whether lead or supporting, Cate was able to instil a sense of truth and vulnerability that allowed her to win over critics and audiences alike. The opportunities in Hollywood cinema did not take long to multiply, and Blanchett began collaborating with some of the most important directors in the industry, from Martin Scorsese to Todd Haynes, proving once again her ability to adapt to all kinds of projects. Her international debut was only the beginning of a career that would continue to surprise for the variety and quality of her performances, making her one of the most respected and admired actresses in the world.

Chapter 4. Consecration with 'Elizabeth

Cate Blanchett's consecration with the film 'Elizabeth' represents one of the most important moments in her career, marking her transition from talented actress to international star. The role of Elizabeth I of England, one of the most complex and fascinating historical characters, required not only remarkable acting skills, but also a deep understanding of the historical and psychological context in which the Queen lived. Cate immersed herself completely in preparing for the role, studying in depth Elizabeth's life and choices, the power dynamics of the English court and the social and political pressures the queen was subjected to. The portrayal of the young queen, who goes from innocence and vulnerability to firmness and cunning, required an intense effort to make this psychological evolution believable. Blanchett was faced with the challenge of embodying a much-loved and revered historical figure, with the added responsibility of balancing her personality with that of the sovereign. The result was a vibrant and extraordinarily human portrait of a queen who, although forced to make brutal choices to maintain power, remained vulnerable in her insecurities and personal feelings.

One of the most challenging aspects of the role was certainly to portray Elizabeth's gradual transformation from an inexperienced young woman, inexperienced in political and emotional matters, to a determined and cool-headed sovereign, willing to sacrifice even her own personal desires for the good of the kingdom. Blanchett was able to interpret this metamorphosis with a delicacy and power that allowed her to convey every single nuance of the character, moving from gentleness to ferocity, from innocence to strategic manipulation. The scenes in which Elizabeth has to deal with betrayal, intrigue and threats to her authority are some of the most intense, and Cate manages to maintain a constant tension, making the audience feel not only the weight of the decisions the queen has to make, but also the inner pain that accompanies them. Blanchett's performance made Elizabeth I a complex and three-dimensional figure, a queen who, behind her façade of strength and control, concealed vulnerabilities and deeply human fears.

The film 'Elizabeth', directed by Shekhar Kapur, not only highlighted Cate's talent, but also played a crucial role in defining her future path as an actress. Prior to this role, Blanchett was mainly known for her theatre work and a few notable film appearances, but 'Elizabeth' was her real stepping stone to global fame. Her ability to dominate the screen with her magnetic presence and her absolute control of the character astounded critics and audiences alike, so much so that her performance was immediately regarded as one of the best of the year. This role not only earned her her first Oscar nomination for Best Actress in a Leading Role, but also marked the beginning of a series of awards and accolades that would define her career for decades to come. Blanchett won a BAFTA, Golden Globe and SAG Award for her performance, further cementing her position as one of the most talented and respected actresses of her generation.

The film's impact on Cate Blanchett's career was immediate and lasting. Before 'Elizabeth', the film industry regarded her as a promising young actress capable of tackling complex and intense roles. After the film, her reputation changed dramatically: she had become a world-class star, one of the few actresses capable of carrying an entire film on her shoulders and making a historical character so vivid and contemporary. Her popularity grew by leaps and bounds, and directors all over the world began to seek her out to offer her ever more prestigious and challenging roles. The success of 'Elizabeth' opened the door to Hollywood for her, where she would go on to work in very high-profile projects, but her choices remained characterised by the same dedication and professionalism that had distinguished her from the beginning.

One of the elements that contributed to the film's success was also the way in which Cate made the character accessible and human, while maintaining her regal status. Elizabeth, as played by Blanchett, is both a majestic figure and a woman struggling with her doubts and fears. This duality made the film an engaging experience, allowing the audience to connect emotionally with the story and to see beyond the image of the distant sovereign, discovering instead a person capable of great sacrifice and difficult decisions. Blanchett managed to strike a perfect balance between the public and private dimensions of the Queen, making her portrait unforgettable.

The success of 'Elizabeth' also had important repercussions on the way Cate Blanchett was perceived in the international film scene. She was no longer just a talented actress, but an iconic figure capable of embodying strong and complex female roles, bringing to the screen a representation of female leadership that was rare for its time. The film itself, with its focus on the power, politics and personal challenges of a queen in a male-dominated world, paid tribute to the strength and resilience of women, themes that would accompany many of her future performances. Thanks to her performance in 'Elizabeth', Blanchett became one of the most sought-after and popular actresses, able to move between art-house films and Hollywood blockbusters with impressive ease.

Her portrayal of Queen Elizabeth remains to this day one of the most celebrated and influential in film history, an example of how a great actress can bring a historical character to the screen and make it relevant to contemporary generations.

Chapter 5. Cate and art-house cinema

Cate Blanchett has always had a strong affinity with auteur cinema, choosing projects that reflect her search for deep and complex roles, and her willingness to collaborate with directors who share a well-defined artistic vision. From the very beginning of her career, Blanchett has been able to balance big-budget films with independent and more experimental films, demonstrating an extraordinary ability to adapt and an inexhaustible curiosity about the language of cinema. Her work with directors of the calibre of Todd Haynes, Jim Jarmusch and Terrence Malick has helped to consolidate her reputation not only as a talented actress, but as a performer who knows how to put herself at the service of complex and sometimes unconventional stories, without ever compromising on quality. Her choices to collaborate with independent authors have been motivated not so much by a desire to gain immediate visibility, but rather by an interest in exploring the emotional and psychological depth of characters, often placed in bold and innovative narrative and stylistic contexts. One of the most significant projects in this sense was the film I'm Not There (2007), directed by Todd Haynes, in which Blanchett played one of the six faces of Bob Dylan. This experimental film, which challenges the conventions of the traditional biopic, was a unique test for the actress. Cate played the androgynous, rebellious version of the legendary musician during the period of his transition from folk music to electric rock. Her extraordinary performance, which saw her not only immerse herself in Dylan's musical and iconographic world, but also embrace an interpretation that challenged genres of identity and representation, earned her unanimous critical acclaim and numerous awards, including the Coppa Volpi at the Venice Film Festival. This performance marked a key moment in her career, demonstrating her ability to tackle extremely complex roles and to adapt to radically different cinematic languages, confirming once again her chameleonic spirit. 'I'm Not There' has become a cult art-house film, and her participation in the project further consolidated her reputation as an artistically committed actress, able to embrace challenges that others might consider too risky.

Her work with director Terrence Malick in 'Knight of Cups' (2015) marked another important milestone in her relationship with art cinema. The film, characterised by a fragmented narrative structure and an almost meditative visual approach, moved away from traditional plots and required actors to put a great deal of effort into interpreting moods and feelings rather than concrete actions. Cate was able to give life to an enigmatic and poignant character, an ex-wife of the protagonist played by Christian Bale, bringing to the screen a performance of rare emotional intensity. Working with a director such as Malick, known for his unconventional method of shooting without a script and his emphasis on images and sensations, was a challenge that Blanchett met with her usual dedication, proving once again her ability to adapt to projects outside the traditional box. Her contribution to the film, albeit in a relatively small role, added a nuance of emotional depth that enriched the work, demonstrating once again her mastery in making each role memorable, regardless of screen time.

The film 'Carol' (2015), also directed by Todd Haynes, was also a perfect example of Cate Blanchett's work in auteur cinema. In this melodrama set in the 1950s, Cate plays Carol Aird, an elegant and sophisticated woman involved in a forbidden love affair with a young photographer, played by Rooney Mara. The film, based on Patricia Highsmith's novel, was a critical success and received numerous awards at international festivals, including the Cannes Film Festival. Blanchett's performance in 'Carol' was praised for its measured elegance and emotional complexity, managing to convey the intensity of the character's desire and suffering with minimalist acting. The film, which delicately and profoundly explores the themes of forbidden love and social repression, reinforced Cate's image as an actress capable of bringing deep, articulate stories steeped in emotional tension to the screen, tackling issues of great social relevance with tact and authenticity.

Cate Blanchett's successes at international festivals testify to the global reach of her impact in auteur cinema. In addition to the awards won for 'I'm Not There' and 'Carol', Blanchett has been a regular at the most prestigious film festivals, from Cannes to Venice, earning her a prominent position not only as an actress, but also as a leading figure in art cinema. Her collaborations with directors such as Alejandro González Iñárritu, in 'Babel' (2006), and Jim Jarmusch, in 'Coffee and Cigarettes' (2003), have contributed to reinforce her image as a sophisticated performer attentive to the most intimate dynamics of film narration. Blanchett has never sought the easiest or most commercial route, always preferring roles that allow her to explore the potential of cinema as an art form and means of expression.

Her impact on contemporary cinema is significant not only for the quality of her performances, but also for her influence in raising the profile of independent films that are often overlooked by the general public. Cate has shown how an internationally renowned actress can balance blockbuster and art house cinema, bringing attention to smaller, less conventional films. This has had a domino effect on the film industry, encouraging other high-profile actors to explore similar projects and support independent cinema.

Cate Blanchett's relationship with art-house cinema represents one of the most fascinating and distinctive aspects of her career. Her ability to choose projects that challenge convention and to work with some of the most innovative and visionary directors of our time has helped redefine the boundaries between commercial and art cinema. Her performances, characterised by deep introspection and a rigorous commitment to the search for emotional truth, have left an indelible mark on contemporary cinema, consolidating her position as one of the most respected and influential actresses of her time.

Chapter 6. The triumphs at the Oscars

Cate Blanchett's Oscar triumphs represent some of the most significant moments of her career, moments that not only confirmed her extraordinary talent, but also redefined the way the film industry perceives high-calibre actresses. Her first Oscar nomination came in 1999, for her extraordinary performance as Queen Elizabeth I in the film 'Elizabeth'. That performance, full of strength, vulnerability and intensity, amazed audiences and critics alike, bringing attention to a young Australian actress who had managed to render a fascinating and modern historical figure. Although that nomination did not result in a win, it was an unmistakable sign that Cate Blanchett would become a constant presence among the world's best actresses. Her name began to circulate in Hollywood circles not only as a promise, but as one of the most versatile and gifted performers of her generation. Even without the Oscar, her reputation was well established, and that nomination marked the beginning of a career that would be studded with accolades and awards.

Her first Oscar win came in 2005, when she won Best Supporting Actress for her role as Katharine Hepburn in Martin Scorsese's The Aviator. This role represented an immense challenge for Cate, not only because it involved playing one of the most iconic figures in film history, but because Hepburn herself had been a multiple Oscar-winning actress, a living legend. However, Cate managed to avoid pure imitation, bringing to the screen a complex and multifaceted version of Hepburn that reflected her eccentricity and charm, but also her frailties. The success of that performance was immediate, and her elegant and modest Oscar acceptance speech was marked by her gratitude to Scorsese and her affirmation of what an honour it was to play a figure like Katharine Hepburn. That victory not only consolidated his position in Hollywood, but also signalled his desire to tackle roles that challenged the expectations and limits of acting, going beyond the simple portrayal of a character.

The most significant triumph of her career came in 2014, when she won the Academy Award for Best Actress in a Leading Role for Woody Allen's 'Blue Jasmine'. Her portrayal of Jasmine French, a disgraced New York socialite grappling with an emotional and psychological crisis, was considered one of the best of the entire decade. Blanchett managed to capture every nuance of the character, oscillating between drama and grotesque, vulnerability and illusion, creating a figure as tragic as she was magnetic. The character of Jasmine was a challenge for any actress, but Cate managed to perfectly balance the character's inner suffering and superficial arrogance, leaving the audience impressed by her ability to convey an entire emotional universe with a simple look or gesture.

During the award ceremony, her acceptance speech was equally memorable: Blanchett emphasised the importance of women's cinema and praised films driven by complex female characters, sending a clear message to the film industry that it was finally beginning to recognise the value of stories told by and about women. That moment was symbolic not only for her personal victory, but also for her influence on an industry that, until then, had often been dominated by male-driven stories.

Cate Blanchett's Oscar wins not only cemented her career, but also had a significant impact on subsequent Oscars and the film industry's perception of her talent. Blanchett has always been a proponent of films that deal with deep themes and complex roles, and her wins helped push the industry towards greater inclusion of stories centred on strong, independent female characters. The focus of her award speeches, in which she spoke passionately about the importance of female representation in film, highlighted her commitment to promoting greater diversity and complexity in women's roles. This had a knock-on effect on the Oscars in the years that followed, with an increased focus on films that focus on women's stories, as well as an encouragement for women directors, screenwriters and producers to make projects that reflected a broader and more inclusive view of the world.

The impact of her Oscar wins was also evident in the way she was perceived by Hollywood. Blanchett became not only an in-demand actress, but also an influential figure on the film scene, able to dictate the rules and choose the roles she found most interesting and challenging, without worrying about commercial conventions. This has allowed her to collaborate with high-calibre directors and continue to work on projects that challenge the norms, proving that Oscar success does not have to translate into more commercial roles, but can be used as a springboard to explore new artistic frontiers. Her impact on the industry has also been felt in her ability to inspire a new generation of actresses, many of whom look to her as a role model for her ability to combine commercial success with artistic depth.

Cate Blanchett's Oscar triumphs have helped shape a career that is now considered one of the most illustrious and respected on the world film scene. Each of her victories, each nomination, has been the result of an unwavering commitment and dedication to her craft, characteristics that have made her one of the most admired and influential actresses of her generation. Her successes at the Oscars are not only individual awards, but also represent the recognition of an entire career dedicated to artistic excellence, the constant search for meaningful roles and the willingness to always push the conventional boundaries of cinema. Blanchett has managed to leave an indelible mark on the Oscars and the entire film industry, setting a new standard of greatness for contemporary actresses.

Chapter 7. Versatility in dramatic and comic roles

Cate Blanchett's versatility in dramatic and comedic roles is one of the elements that has defined her extraordinary career, making her one of the most appreciated and respected actresses worldwide. Her ability to switch seamlessly between intense, deep characters and light, ironic interpretations is a testament to her absolute mastery of the craft and her inclination to not limit herself to one genre. Her career is studded with roles ranging from the darkest and most complex dramas to the brightest comedies, without the quality of her performance suffering as a result. Cate has always chosen to tackle each character with the same commitment and emotional quest, regardless of the tone of the film or the genre. This ability to play such diverse roles has made her a reference point for colleagues and critics, who see in her a rare example of artistic adaptability.

Throughout her career, Blanchett has tackled dramatic roles of great emotional intensity, which required complete immersion in the character and an extraordinary sensitivity in rendering the subtlest nuances of human emotion. One of the most famous examples is certainly her performance in 'Blue Jasmine' (2013), where she plays a woman who faces an emotional and psychological breakdown after the loss of her social status and marriage. Jasmine is a complex character, tormented by her arrogance and frailties, and Cate manages to masterfully capture every facet of her psyche, moving from moments of despair to brief bursts of lucidity, all with a believability that only an actress of her stature can achieve. Her methodical approach to acting, characterised by in-depth character analysis, allows her to bring to the screen a range of emotions that never leaves the viewer indifferent. Her performance in 'Blue Jasmine' earned her numerous awards, including the Oscar for Best Actress in a Leading Role, confirming her ability to dominate dramatic roles.

Alongside these more serious and complex roles, Cate Blanchett has also shown an extraordinary ability to cast herself in comic characters, displaying a surprising lightness and comic vis. In films such as 'The Monuments Men' (2014) and 'Thor: Ragnarok' (2017), she has been able to give performances that combine her innate elegance with a brilliant and cutting humour. The character of Hela in 'Thor: Ragnarok', despite being an antagonist in an action film, is characterised by an ironic streak that Cate was able to play to perfection, playing with her natural charisma and her ability to make a villain not only threatening, but also charming and funny. In these comic performances, Blanchett demonstrates a mastery of timing and tone that is not easy to find in actors used mainly to dramatic roles. Her ability to switch from gravity to levity without losing authenticity is one of the secrets of her success and one of the characteristics that make her one of the most complete performers on the contemporary film scene.

Another aspect of her versatility emerges in characters that straddle the line between drama and comedy, those roles that require a balance between emotional depth and narrative levity. A perfect example of this is her performance in 'Carol' (2015), a film that, although dramatic, feeds on delicate nuances and intimate moments that require sensitivity and a light touch. Cate managed to play Carol with a grace that allowed her to make the character as powerful as she is vulnerable, demonstrating how an actress can mix different interpretative registers in a single performance without ever seeming out of place. Carol, a woman fighting for her freedom and her love in an age of repression, is a character steeped in silences and unspoken gestures, and Blanchett manages to make every look and every word loaded with meaning, combining her dramatic mastery with her ability to lighten the scene with a simple inflection of her voice or a subtle smile.

Cate Blanchett's ability to adapt to such diverse roles has not gone unnoticed. Critics have always praised her versatility, praising her for her ability to make believable characters who experience extreme and often diametrically opposed situations. It is not easy for an actor to be believable in deeply dramatic roles as well as in light or even grotesque ones, but Blanchett has shown that she can excel in both fields. The awards and accolades she has received throughout her career are tangible proof of this ability. Not only has she won numerous Oscars, Golden Globes and BAFTAs, but she is also one of the few actresses to have been nominated for roles in so many different genres, demonstrating an artistic flexibility that few can boast. Her bold choices in film have also had a profound influence on many of her colleagues, who see in her an example of dedication and openness to projects that are not confined to the boundaries of traditional acting.

The directors she has worked with have also pointed out that her versatility is one of the characteristics that makes her one of the most sought-after actresses in the world. Cate's ability to understand the director's vision and adapt to the tone of the film is a rare quality that allows her to work in extremely different contexts and always manage to bring something new and personal to each character. Her influence also extends to the audience, who see in her an actress capable of making the most diverse experiences human and understandable. Thanks to this adaptability, Cate Blanchett has expanded the boundaries of what an actress can do on screen, proving that versatility is not only a desirable quality, but an art in itself, capable of making each performance unique and memorable.

Cate Blanchett's versatility in dramatic and comedic roles is one of her most extraordinary and distinctive qualities. Her approach to complex characters, which requires intense and deep work, is combined with her ability to tackle light roles with the same precision and dedication. This makes her one of the most accomplished performers of her generation, capable of turning each role into an engaging experience, both for the audience and for those who work with her. Blanchett has proven that adaptability is one of the keys to success in an ever-changing industry, and her example continues to inspire actors, directors and audiences worldwide.

Chapter 8. The performance in 'Blue Jasmine

Cate Blanchett's performance in 'Blue Jasmine' (2013) was one of the high points of her career, a role that represented an unprecedented emotional and technical challenge. In the film directed by Woody Allen, Blanchett plays Jasmine French, a New York high society woman who loses everything after her husband's financial scandal and moves to San Francisco, trying to rebuild her life amidst an increasingly evident psychological crisis. Jasmine's character is complex and layered, characterised by a fragility that hides behind an appearance of superiority and sophistication. Blanchett's greatest challenge was to maintain a balance between the character's superficial elegance and her inner disintegration, a task that required extraordinary acting skills and a deep understanding of the psychological dynamics that drive Jasmine towards self-deception and emotional collapse.

One of the main difficulties in tackling this role was the fact that Jasmine is not an easy character to like or pity. Her arrogance, her sense of superiority and the way she treats anyone who does not belong to her own world make her, at least at first, an unempathetic character. However, Blanchett managed to find a space of vulnerability and desperation that allowed the audience to see beyond her façade, revealing a woman destroyed by her own illusions. Jasmine lives in a world built on lies, first the lies of her husband, an unscrupulous businessman who has ruined many people's lives, and then the lies she tells herself to try to maintain an image of perfection that is crumbling. Her inability to adapt to a new reality, far from the luxury and comfort she was accustomed to, collides with a mental deterioration that takes her further and further towards the abyss. Blanchett, with her calibrated and masterful acting, was able to make every nuance of this fall believable, keeping the audience gripped even in the most difficult and painful moments of the narrative.

Working with a director like Woody Allen represented a great opportunity for Cate Blanchett, but also a significant challenge. Allen is known for his particular approach to directing, which often gives the actors a lot of freedom, but also requires a capacity for improvisation and a keen sense of comic and dramatic timing. For a role like Jasmine, this approach allowed Blanchett to fully explore the character's psychology, to play with the silences, nervous gestures and emotional outbursts that characterise Jasmine, making her not only a victim of circumstance, but also partly the architect of her own downfall. The interaction with the other characters, in particular with her sister Ginger, played by Sally Hawkins, created moments of great emotional tension, where the distance between Jasmine's idealised world and Ginger's simpler, more genuine reality is clearly perceived. Allen

41

allowed Blanchett to experiment with her character, resulting in a performance that is both tragic and, at times, even grotesque.

The emotional impact of the character on Cate Blanchett herself was remarkable. In several interviews, the actress has spoken of how challenging it was to live Jasmine's pain and despair day after day during filming. Jasmine is a woman who has lost everything: money, social standing, love and, finally, her sanity. Bringing all this to the screen required Blanchett to dig deep within herself to find the raw and painful emotions that make the character so authentic. Jasmine's inner tension manifests itself in every scene, through her rigid body language, her distant gaze and her nervous hands, always trying to control a world that is getting out of hand. Blanchett has succeeded in bringing to life on screen a complex character who is caught between the desire to find her past life and the growing realisation that that world is now lost forever.

Cate Blanchett's performance in 'Blue Jasmine' was immediately acclaimed by critics, who recognised the depth and skill of her performance. Her ability to bring to life a character so tragic, yet so human, struck a deep chord with audiences. The awards and accolades were not long in coming: Blanchett won virtually every award available for Best Actress in a Leading Role, from the Golden Globe to the BAFTA to the Oscar. Winning the Oscar for Best

Actress in a Leading Role was an important moment not only for Blanchett's career, but also for the recognition of the importance of complex female roles in contemporary cinema. In her acceptance speech, Blanchett thanked Woody Allen for the trust placed in her and emphasised the importance of making films centred on strong, multifaceted female characters, sending a clear message to the film industry to continue to support stories that focus on complex and flawed, yet deeply human women.

'Blue Jasmine' also had a significant impact on the way Cate Blanchett was perceived globally. If before the film she was already considered one of the most talented actresses of her generation, after this performance she became a true icon, capable of tackling extremely difficult roles and making them accessible to the general public without ever sacrificing the emotional or psychological complexity of the character. Jasmine French is a character who remains imprinted for her disarming humanity, and Blanchett's performance was one of the most memorable of the entire decade, capable of influencing not only audiences, but also many actors and directors who saw in her a model of artistic perfection.

The character of Jasmine, with all her frailties, fears and illusions, has become a symbol of how cinema can explore the human psyche and bring to the screen stories that reflect our deepest vulnerabilities. Blanchett, with her performance, created a character that will forever remain in the history of cinema, a woman who struggles against herself and the world, and who, despite her descent into madness, remains incredibly real and close.

Chapter 9. Passion for theatre and directing

Cate Blanchett's passion for theatre has been a constant in her career, an inexhaustible source of inspiration and an anchor of artistic authenticity, even when her film fame led her to work on Hollywood sets. Blanchett has never considered the theatre merely as an initial stage in her acting career, but as a place to which she has returned again and again to hone her craft and test herself in a context that requires total discipline and dedication. One of the most significant moments of this connection to theatre was her engagement as co-artistic director of the Sydney Theatre Company (STC), which she shared with her husband, Andrew Upton, from 2008 to 2013. This role represented not only an opportunity for Blanchett to lead one of Australia's most important theatrical institutions, but also the chance to directly influence the international theatre scene, pursuing an ambitious programme that blended tradition and innovation. During her tenure, Blanchett has demonstrated a clear and bold vision, choosing to stage revisited classic works and contemporary texts, bringing new authors and directors to work with the company, and constantly seeking to challenge audiences with bold artistic choices.

Cate Blanchett's experience as a theatre director was a natural evolution of her career, enriched by the experience accumulated over the years as an actress. Directing for the theatre was a different challenge than acting, as it requires an overall eye for the whole project, not only for one's own character. Her directing has always been characterised by a deep concern for the actors' work, trying to help them find the emotional truth in their characters, similar to the way she has always approached acting. One of the most significant projects she directed at the Sydney Theatre Company was 'The War of the Roses', an ambitious Shakespearean adaptation that condensed four historical plays into one epic production. In this project, Blanchett worked as both actress and director, showing her ability to balance two very challenging roles and bring a powerful and cohesive vision to the stage. Her approach to directing is distinguished by her sensitivity to text and attention to detail, qualities she inherited from her experience as an actress, but which she has been able to hone and apply successfully in a new capacity.

One of the most fascinating aspects of her theatrical career is the way she has been able to combine her film activity with the theatre. Despite being one of the most sought-after actresses in Hollywood, Blanchett has never given up the stage, always finding the time and energy to return to the theatre, even at times when her film career was at its peak. The difference between film and theatre, for Blanchett, is evident both technically and emotionally. Theatre, with its immediacy and direct contact with the audience, offers an experience that cinema cannot replicate: each performance is unique and unrepeatable, each night different from the next, and the energy that is created between actors and spectators is something intangible but fundamental to the success of a performance. Film, on the other hand, is an art form that allows greater control over the performance, thanks to the long lead times and the possibility of repeating scenes until the desired perfection is achieved. However, it is precisely the element of risk and vulnerability that characterises theatre that makes it so attractive to Cate. In theatre, there is no room for error: every word, every gesture must be perfect at the right moment, and this level of constant pressure is what, according to Blanchett, keeps actors sharp and alive.

Her artistic legacy in theatre is already significant, not only because of the memorable roles she has played on stage, but also because of the impact she has had as an artistic director and director. Under her leadership, the Sydney Theatre Company has seen a revival that has taken the company to a level of international recognition never before achieved. Blanchett has managed to forge collaborations with theatres around the world, taking STC productions on international tours that have enabled audiences in New York, London and Paris to appreciate the talent and creativity of the Australian company. This cultural exchange has enriched not only the company, but also Blanchett herself, who has been able to engage with a variety of theatre styles and traditions, further expanding her artistic vocabulary. Her ability to attract big names in international theatre, both actors and directors, has helped to raise the quality of productions and make the Sydney Theatre Company one of the most innovative and respected companies in the world.

But Cate Blanchett's legacy in theatre goes beyond simply directing or playing great roles. Her dedication to this art form, her commitment to fostering new talent and her willingness to constantly experiment with new theatrical forms and languages have made her a figurehead for many generations of actors and directors. Blanchett has always believed in the power of theatre as a place for social and political reflection, a means of interrogating society and exploring the universal themes that run through our lives. In her years at the Sydney Theatre Company, she staged plays that addressed contemporary issues such as social inequality, women's rights and the environmental crisis, proving that theatre is not only a place of entertainment, but also a powerful tool for change and awareness.

Cate Blanchett's passion for theatre and directing is a fundamental part of her artistic identity. Although she has achieved international success as a film actress, Blanchett has always considered theatre to be the beating heart of her career, a place where she can explore new challenges, take risks and grow as an artist. Her commitment to directing the Sydney Theatre Company has left an indelible mark on the company's history and helped strengthen the role of Australian theatre on the world stage. Her artistic legacy will continue to influence and inspire actors and directors for years to come, cementing her role not only as one of the most talented actresses of her generation, but also as one of the most influential and innovative figures in contemporary theatre.

Chapter 10. An icon of fashion and style

Cate Blanchett is considered an international fashion and style icon, not only for her undisputed talent as an actress, but also for her ability to embody elegance in every public appearance. Over the years, she has developed an ever-evolving personal style, managing to combine sophistication, boldness and refinement with a disarming naturalness. Her attention to detail, her awareness of her own body and her ability to adapt clothes to any context have made her a reference figure for stylists, fashion critics and fans the world over. Since her early days in film, Blanchett has demonstrated impeccable taste, choosing outfits that did not simply follow the trends of the moment, but reflected her unique personality and her approach to art and fashion. Her preference for elegant, minimalist looks, alternating with more experimental and daring choices, helped create an aesthetic that became instantly recognisable and admired.

The evolution of her personal style has been influenced by a variety of factors, including her film career and her experiences in the world of theatre. At the beginning of her career, Cate favoured classic, understated clothes, which enhanced her slender figure and regal bearing. But as the years went by and her public image was consolidated, she began to dare more, opting for garments with bold and innovative lines, often experimenting with unusual colours, textures and cuts. This stylistic evolution reflected not only her personal growth, but also her desire to use fashion as a means of artistic expression, rather than mere adornment. Blanchett has always considered fashion as an extension of her creative work, a way to play roles outside the set, playing with identities and symbols through the clothes she chooses to wear.

Cate Blanchett's collaborations with major fashion houses have been instrumental in defining her as a global style icon. Over the years, she has worked with some of the world's most celebrated designers and brands, including Armani, Givenchy, Valentino, Gucci and Alexander McQueen, becoming a muse for many of them. One of her closest ties is with Giorgio Armani, for whom she has been an ambassador and the face of advertising campaigns for several years. Armani's refined, elegant and timeless style perfectly matches Cate's personality, and her role as brand ambassador has helped consolidate her image as a woman of class and good taste. At the same time, Blanchett has also shown an ability to embrace the innovative spirit of bolder brands, such as Alexander McQueen, with his sculptural and sometimes provocative clothes, and Gucci, with its eccentric creations full of artistic detailing.

One of the most admired aspects of her style is her ability to interpret each outfit with grace and naturalness. Whether it is a couture dress worn on the red carpet at the Cannes Film Festival or a casual outfit for a press conference, Cate always manages to maintain an impeccable presence and bring the clothes she wears to life, making them unique and personal. Her style is never banal, but neither is it ostentatious: even in her boldest choices, Blanchett manages to maintain a balance between originality and sophistication, avoiding any excess and always looking extremely sophisticated. This ability to carry an innate sense of elegance has secured her a place among the most admired women in the fashion world.

Cate Blanchett's impact on international trends has been significant. Her style choices have often influenced the fashion world, bringing attention to new designers or helping to launch trends that have since caught on globally. His red carpet looks are constantly the focus of the industry media, and each of his appearances is awaited with curiosity by stylists, critics and fans. Her style has also had an important cultural impact, as it represents an idea of femininity that does not simply follow traditional conventions. Blanchett has always shown that fashion can also be a tool of empowerment, capable of conveying messages of strength, intelligence and independence. In an industry often dominated by stereotypes and superficial expectations, Cate has been able to construct a different narrative, where clothing becomes an integral part of her artistic expression and complex personality.

The fashion world has recognised Cate Blanchett's contribution with numerous awards and accolades, cementing her status as a style icon. She has often been included in rankings of the world's best dressed women by prestigious fashion magazines such as Vogue, Harper's Bazaar and Vanity Fair. But more than the awards, it is the respect she has earned in the industry that testifies to her lasting impact. Blanchett is appreciated not only for her impeccable appearance, but also for her intelligence and the way she uses fashion to express her point of view. Even in the most formal settings, such as the Oscars ceremony or other glamorous events, Cate has always been able to bring a dimension of authenticity and personality, ensuring that her looks reflect who she is as a person, rather than simply being a showcase for expensive clothes.

One of the key elements of her approach to fashion is also her focus on ethics and sustainability. In recent years, Cate has shown a strong commitment to promoting more conscious fashion, choosing to wear clothes from designers who adopt sustainable practices or reusing red carpet dresses for different occasions, thus sending an important message about the importance of responsible consumption even in an industry such as luxury fashion. This commitment has further reinforced her public image as a conscious and globally aware woman who uses her visibility to support important causes. Cate Blanchett has become a fashion and style icon thanks to her ability to constantly evolve, her collaboration with major fashion houses and her impact on international trends. Her image, characterised by elegance, sophistication and innovation, has profoundly influenced the fashion industry, inspiring designers and fans worldwide. Recognised and admired for her impeccable style, Blanchett has managed to turn every public appearance into a fashion event, consolidating her status as a timeless icon, capable of fusing art and fashion into a unique and authentic expression of her personality.

Chapter 11. The connection with Australia

Cate Blanchett's connection with Australia has always been deep and fundamental, both in her personal life and in her artistic career. Although she has achieved an international fame that has led her to work with some of the world's greatest directors and actors, Australia has always been a reference point for her, a place where she has been able to root her art and identity. Growing up in the suburbs of Melbourne, Blanchett has always felt the influence of Australian culture on her life, particularly in the way the country has shaped her approach to work and creativity. Australia's open, dynamic and free environment, far from the pressures and rigid patterns of Hollywood, has given Cate the opportunity to explore her own artistic expression in a context that values authenticity and innovation. This background has had a significant impact not only on her career, but also on the kind of artist she has become: a professional who always seeks to challenge the boundaries of art, experimenting with new languages and approaches, without being afraid to take risks.

One of the most important aspects of this connection is her constant return to Australian theatre, which for her has always represented a place of great personal and artistic growth. Having trained at the National Institute of Dramatic Art (NIDA) in Sydney,

Blanchett has always maintained a strong connection to the world of theatre in her home country, often returning to Australian stages, even when her film career was at its peak. The theatre, for Blanchett, is a sacred place where the actor can truly explore his craft without the distractions or superstructures of film. This periodic return to Australian theatre has not only been a way of staying connected to her roots, but also a way of giving something back to the local arts community by sharing the experiences and skills she has gained internationally. Cate has always sought to bring to Australian audiences not only classic works, but also innovative and experimental shows, helping to raise the level of national theatre and bringing new perspectives on the performing arts to the country.

Australia's cultural influence on his career has also manifested itself through his active involvement in promoting and supporting the arts in the country. During her time as co-artistic director of the Sydney Theatre Company (STC) with her husband Andrew Upton, Blanchett has had a huge impact on the arts in Australia. Her work has helped strengthen the position of Australian theatre on the international stage, creating a bridge between Australia and the world, leading the company to perform in major international theatres. This role enabled her to promote a type of theatre that was innovative, inclusive and open to new trends, bringing young local talent to the fore and providing a platform for artistic experimentation. During her tenure, Blanchett staged not only great classics, but also contemporary works that reflected the social and political concerns of the time, demonstrating a strong commitment to current events and issues affecting Australian society.

Her connection with the local arts community was equally significant. Blanchett has always maintained a deep respect and affection for Australian artists, whom she considers part of an extended family. Even when working on international film sets, her heart was always turned towards Australia, where she regularly returned not only to work, but also to live and contribute to the cultural growth of the country. Through her presence and commitment, Blanchett has influenced and inspired many generations of young Australian actors, directors and creatives, who see in her a model of professionalism and dedication. She has become a symbol of how an artist can achieve global success while maintaining a strong connection to her roots. On numerous occasions she has also emphasised the importance of supporting local culture and arts institutions, recognising how crucial it is for a country's growth to invest in the arts.

Blanchett has also been an important voice in defending and promoting Australia's cultural identity around the world. She has often spoken about the diversity and cultural richness of her country, emphasising how Australia, with its complex history and indigenous roots, offers a unique perspective on the world. This aspect of her Australian identity has led her to support projects that highlight the stories and experiences of Australia's indigenous communities, helping to give voice to narratives that are often ignored or marginalised. Cate has always seen her role as an artist not only in terms of performance, but also as an opportunity to amplify voices that deserve to be heard, and Australia has provided a context in which this type of engagement has been particularly meaningful. His dedication to promoting the arts in his country has had a lasting impact, helping to strengthen Australia's recognition as a vital centre for creativity and innovation.

Her love for Australia and her commitment to supporting its culture never waned, even as her international career exploded. Blanchett has always found ways to return home, connect with her homeland and contribute to its artistic development. For her, Australia is not just a physical place, but an inexhaustible source of inspiration and strength. Her Australian roots have influenced the way she approaches acting, directing and her role in the world of film and theatre. This deep connection has allowed Blanchett to maintain a sense of balance and authenticity in her career, without ever losing sight of what is truly important: artistic integrity and respect for her work. In this way, Cate Blanchett has left an indelible mark not only on international cinema, but also on the Australian arts, becoming a symbol of excellence and dedication to her home country.

Through her involvement in Australian theatre, her work with the local arts community and her constant promotion of her country's culture, Blanchett has shown that it is possible to achieve international success without ever forgetting one's roots. Her contribution to the arts in Australia has been extraordinary, and her impact will surely be felt for many years to come, both locally and globally.

Chapter 12. The role of Galadriel in 'Lord of the Rings

The role of Galadriel in Lord of the Rings was one of the most iconic moments in Cate Blanchett's career, leading her to play a figure of immense power and grace in one of the most beloved and influential film franchises of all time. Blanchett's preparation for the character was rigorous and thorough, a process that saw her fully immerse herself in the universe created by J.R.R. Tolkien and the mythology of Arda. Galadriel is one of the oldest and most powerful figures in Middle-earth, an immortal elf who carries with her not only the wisdom of millennia, but also a profound knowledge of the dark forces that threaten the world. Playing such a complex and mystical character required a subtle understanding of her personality and her role in the larger context of the story. Blanchett studied Tolkien's texts with great care, trying to capture Galadriel's essence, her connection to nature, her sense of responsibility for the fate of Middle-earth and her immense power, held with dignified calm.

Director Peter Jackson helped create an environment in which Blanchett could explore the character in depth, and the result was a performance that left its mark not only on the hearts of fans of the book, but also on the wider film audience. Galadriel appears as an ethereal, almost otherworldly figure, a character who exudes an aura of wisdom and power, but who also manages to convey a deep humanity, especially in her interactions with other characters, such as Frodo and Gandalf. Blanchett brought a magnetic presence to Galadriel, a mixture of authority and grace that perfectly embodies the character's immortality and wisdom. The greatest challenge was probably balancing the sense of wonder and power that Galadriel inspires with her vulnerability and inner doubt. The moment in which Galadriel rejects the Ring of Power, choosing to remain true to her nature rather than give in to the temptation of absolute domination, is one of the trilogy's key moments and shows the character's moral depth, a quality Blanchett was able to render with incredible emotional force.

The cultural impact of The Lord of the Rings trilogy has been immense, and the character of Galadriel has played a key role in this success. The trilogy is not only one of the most awarded and appreciated film sagas, but has also created a real movement of fans, fascinated by Tolkien's rich and detailed world and the masterful performances of the actors involved. Blanchett was able to make Galadriel an iconic figure in the pantheon of fantasy cinema, and her portrayal of the elf helped redefine the female role in the genre. In a cinematic world often dominated by male heroes, Galadriel emerges as a strong, independent and charismatic presence who plays a crucial role in the destiny of Middle-earth without ever being reduced to a mere extra. Her power derives not from physical strength, but from her wisdom, her intelligence and her deep connection to nature and the fate of the world. At a time when the representation of women in the media was beginning to change, Galadriel became a symbol of female power, a figure who embodies a quiet but unstoppable force.

Fan reception was enthusiastic, and Galadriel quickly became one of the most beloved characters in the film trilogy. Tolkien fans were initially concerned that the character's complexity and majesty might be difficult to render on screen, but Blanchett exceeded all expectations, delivering a performance that was both true to the spirit of the book and innovative in the cinematic context. Fans praised her ability to convey all of Galadriel's history and wisdom with just a few gestures and words, and her performance became a benchmark for subsequent portrayals of powerful, mythical figures in fantasy cinema. Her version of Galadriel has inspired fans around the world, and her image has been reproduced in endless merchandising items, making the character not only an integral part of the film trilogy, but also of contemporary pop culture.

The legacy of Galadriel's character is still very much alive today, and Cate Blanchett has contributed significantly to cementing her place in film history. Galadriel has become a symbol of wisdom, power and beauty, a figure that transcends time and space, much like the character herself within Tolkien's mythology. Blanchett has managed to make the character not only memorable, but also a source of inspiration for many women, inside and outside the world of film. Her portrayal of Galadriel has influenced the way powerful female characters have been portrayed subsequently, helping to shift the focus to strong and complex women, not defined by their ties to men, but by their choices, their morality and their ability to face the most difficult challenges.

Moreover, the impact of her performance extended far beyond the boundaries of cinema. Galadriel has also been a central figure in other works inspired by Tolkien's universe, and Blanchett's image has often been associated with the character in such portrayals. Even in new productions linked to the Middle-earth mythology, such as The Rings of Power, the figure of Galadriel continues to evoke the solemn and imposing portrait that Blanchett created, leaving an indelible imprint in the minds of audiences and in subsequent generations of actors and filmmakers who engage with this rich material. The role of Galadriel represented one of the greatest and most rewarding challenges of her career for Cate Blanchett, an opportunity to embody a complex and fascinating character in an epic cinematic context. Her performance left an indelible imprint on both the film world and popular culture, cementing her place among the greatest actresses of her generation and making Galadriel one of the most iconic and beloved characters in modern fantasy. The way Blanchett brought this role to life showed her extraordinary ability to combine emotional depth with a magnetic stage presence, making Galadriel an immortal figure in the hearts of viewers around the world.

Chapter 13. Successes in independent cinema

Cate Blanchett is known for her ability to alternate roles in big blockbusters with smaller, more committed projects, demonstrating a constant inclination towards independent cinema. This aspect of her career reflects her deep dedication to acting as an art form, rather than simply as a means to commercial success. Blanchett has always chosen scripts with care and, on many occasions, has preferred to work in low-budget productions that allowed her to explore more complex and multifaceted roles, far from the constraints of mass Hollywood productions. Independent cinema has offered her the freedom to explore controversial or personal issues, often with a more experimental cinematic language that is less tied to market logic. These choices have had a considerable impact not only on her career, but also on the perception that the public and the critics have of her as an actress: a professional who is not afraid to immerse herself in difficult or controversial roles, always searching for authenticity and depth in the characters she plays.

One of Cate Blanchett's first significant successes in independent cinema was 'Coffee and Cigarettes' (2003), an episodic film directed by Jim Jarmusch. In this film, Blanchett plays two roles, herself and an imaginary cousin, in a dialogue that highlights the contrasts between success and failure, fame and real life. This project highlighted her ability to move with ease from mainstream to art-house cinema, while maintaining the same intensity and dedication. The collaboration with Jarmusch, a director known for his unconventional and minimalist approach, marked one of the key moments in her relationship with independent cinema, pushing her towards a career that would balance commercial films with more intimate and risky artistic projects. 'Coffee and Cigarettes' also demonstrated Blanchett's versatility in creating two distinct characters within the same film, delivering a subtle and ironic performance that won over critics.

Another important example of her involvement in independent cinema is the film 'I'm Not There' (2007), directed by Todd Haynes. In this experimental film, Blanchett played one of the six faces of Bob Dylan, in a multifaceted portrait of the legendary singer-songwriter. Her portrayal of Dylan, in a role that defied all conventions of gender and identity, captured the attention of audiences and critics alike. The film was a hit at international festivals and showed how Blanchett was willing to push the boundaries of traditional acting to explore new artistic horizons. Her performance earned her numerous awards, including the Coppa Volpi at the Venice Film Festival and an Oscar nomination for Best Supporting Actress. The role in I'm Not There was a turning point in her career, cementing her reputation as a bold and innovative actress, ready to tackle scripts that require total immersion and a flair for exploring the ambiguity and complexity of characters.

Over the years, Blanchett has continued to choose independent projects that allow her to tackle important social and political issues, as in the case of 'Carol' (2015), a film directed by Todd Haynes that tells the forbidden love story between two women in the 1950s. Based on the novel by Patricia Highsmith, 'Carol' is a delicate and refined work, in which Blanchett played the role of a sophisticated woman but trapped in the rigid social conventions of the time. The film, made on a modest budget compared to Hollywood blockbusters, was an extraordinary success at independent film festivals and received several Oscar nominations. Blanchett's performance was considered one of the best of her career, praised for her elegance and the emotional complexity she brought to the character of Carol Aird. This role once again demonstrated Blanchett's ability to play complex characters, capable of communicating entire inner worlds with a simple expression or glance. 'Carol' had a significant impact not only on Blanchett's career, but also on the representation of same-sex relationships in mainstream cinema, helping to shift the public discourse towards greater inclusion and acceptance of diversity.

The impact of independent cinema on Cate Blanchett's career was also decisive in terms of her future choices. Working in low-budget productions and collaborating with directors who prioritised artistic exploration over commercial success allowed her to hone her ability to select projects that went beyond simply playing a role. Blanchett has always favoured scripts that address universal themes, but do so through a personal and original lens, allowing audiences to see new facets of the human condition. This predisposition has influenced the way she has built her career, avoiding being labelled into one type of role or film genre. Instead, she has built a reputation as an actress capable of bringing emotional and intellectual depth to any project, regardless of the size of the production.

Her experience in independent cinema has also been reflected in her approach to major commercial films. Cate Blanchett has always shown that success should not be defined by a film's budget or box-office potential, but by its ability to touch deep emotional chords and push the audience to reflect. This approach has also influenced her choices in blockbusters, where she has continued to look for roles that have a deeper meaning and that allow her to explore new nuances in her acting. Even in films like 'Thor: Ragnarok' (2017), in which she plays the role of Hela, Blanchett was able to bring an intensity and complexity that surprised audiences, proving that even in a commercial context it is possible to play rich and multifaceted characters.

Cate Blanchett's journey into independent cinema has been a crucial part of her career and development as an actress. Through challenging roles and daring scripts, she has helped redefine the way audiences perceive art-house cinema and brought a breath of authenticity and innovation to the world of cinema. Her ability to navigate between projects of different scales, always maintaining a very high level of professionalism and creativity, has allowed her to leave an indelible mark on both independent and commercial cinema. The choices she has made throughout her career are a testament to her commitment to promoting the artistic value of cinema, demonstrating that, regardless of the size of the project, what really counts is the truth that one manages to bring to the screen.

Chapter 14. Social and environmental commitment

Cate Blanchett is known not only for her extraordinary talent as an actress, but also for her social and environmental commitment, which has played a significant role in shaping her public image. Over the years, Blanchett has supported various humanitarian and environmental causes, with a particular focus on combating climate change and promoting sustainability. Her dedication to these issues is not limited to mere token support, but is rooted in a deep conviction that individuals, particularly those with visibility and influence such as herself, have a responsibility to the planet and future generations. One of the most important battles Blanchett has devoted time and energy to is the fight against climate change. Over the past decades, she has worked with various international organisations, trying to raise awareness among the public and governments about the urgency of taking action to reduce carbon emissions and tackle global environmental crises. Her commitment has been visible through numerous initiatives, both in the Australian context and globally, which have seen her at the forefront as an activist and advocate for sustainability.

One of Cate Blanchett's most significant collaborations has been with the Australian Conservation Foundation (ACF), one of the most important environmental organisations in Australia. Blanchett has been one of the most influential voices in advocating the importance of switching to renewable energy sources and reducing dependence on fossil fuels, a problem particularly acute in her home country, known for its coal mining and extraction industry. In 2007, Blanchett and her husband Andrew Upton spearheaded a campaign to make the Sydney Theatre Company (STC), of which they were co-directors, one of the first theatres in the world to be completely powered by renewable energy. This project was a concrete example of how environmental commitment can be integrated into cultural and artistic activities, demonstrating that it is possible to combine artistic excellence and sustainability. The transformation of the STC into a green theatre has had a strong media impact, bringing to the public's attention the importance of taking concrete action to reduce the carbon footprint and demonstrating that cultural institutions can also play a leading role in the fight against climate change.

In addition to her work in Australia, Blanchett has worked with international organisations such as the United Nations Refugee Council (UNHCR), for which she has been a Goodwill Ambassador since 2016. In this role, she has actively supported the cause of refugees, bringing to light the plight of millions of people forced to leave their homes due to conflict, persecution and environmental disasters. One of the hallmarks of her work with UNHCR has been a focus on the connection between climate change and the refugee crisis. Blanchett highlighted how environmental degradation and rising temperatures are exacerbating global inequalities and forcing entire populations to migrate. She has visited refugee camps in different parts of the world, including Jordan and Bangladesh, documenting the living conditions of refugees and seeking to raise international awareness of the urgency of finding humanitarian and ecological solutions to these interconnected crises. His work with the UNHCR has not been limited to symbolic interventions or public statements, but has involved a personal and ongoing commitment, putting his notoriety at the service of one of the most pressing humanitarian causes of our time.

Cate Blanchett's environmental and social commitment has also influenced her professional choices. In recent years, the actress has also shown an increasing focus on sustainability in her public appearances, choosing to wear clothes made by designers who adopt ecological and sustainable practices. Blanchett was among the first celebrities to wear the same dress several times on different red carpets, sending a clear message against the excessive consumerism that often characterises the fashion industry. This seemingly simple gesture became a symbolic act of resistance against the culture of waste and fast fashion, emphasising how personal choices can also contribute to wider change. This approach to sustainability has further reinforced her public image as a coherent and conscious figure, able to use her influence to promote ethical and responsible values.

Moreover, her commitment has had a significant impact on public and media perceptions of her. Blanchett is seen as an actress who not only excels in her work, but is actively committed to causes beyond the world of film. Her ability to balance career and activism has shown that celebrities can and should use their platform to raise awareness for issues of global importance. This has helped make Blanchett a figure admired not only for her talent, but also for her courage in taking a stand on complex and controversial issues. The fact that she has chosen to support issues such as climate change and refugee rights, often polarising topics, has demonstrated her willingness to go beyond the role of a mere testimonial, engaging in public debate with a clear and responsible vision.

The influence of her social and environmental commitment also extends to future generations of actors and artists. Blanchett has inspired many colleagues and young talents to get involved in humanitarian causes, proving that it is possible to reconcile a successful career with a life dedicated to the common good. Her ability to speak knowledgeably and passionately about complex issues has made her a respected figure not only in the entertainment industry, but also among activists and global leaders. Through her visibility and unwavering commitment, Blanchett has helped bring greater prominence to issues that are often overlooked by the mainstream media, advancing a broader discourse on the need for collective action to address the environmental and social challenges of our time.

Through her work with the UNHCR, her support for renewable energy and her constant promotion of sustainability, Blanchett has shown that celebrities can have a real and lasting impact on society. Her example of dedication and responsibility will continue to inspire both her colleagues and the public, showing that change can start even from small personal actions, amplified by notoriety and the power to influence consciences.

Chapter 15. Private and family life

Cate Blanchett's private life has always been an aspect of her existence that the actress has managed with great discretion, maintaining a delicate balance between her extraordinary career in show business and her roles as wife and mother. Since 1997, Blanchett has been married to Andrew Upton, an Australian playwright and director, with whom she has built a strong bond and a family that remains the focus of her personal life. Cate and Andrew's relationship has been characterised by a deep complicity, both in private life and at work, as the two have shared numerous professional projects, including co-directing the Sydney Theatre Company. This collaboration has been a key part of their lives together, combining their creative passions in a work context that has further strengthened their bond. Blanchett has always spoken of Upton with great affection and respect, describing him as a stable presence and supportive partner, able to balance the challenges of career and family management with her.

Despite the visibility and work commitments of both, Cate Blanchett and Andrew Upton have chosen to keep their private lives out of the spotlight, trying to protect their intimacy and that of their children. The couple has four children: Dashiell, Roman, Ignatius and Edith. The balance between career and family has always been a central theme for Blanchett, who has often stated how important it is for her to maintain a strong bond with her children and create a stable family environment, despite her work commitments that often take her away from home. The role of mother is one of the most important aspects of her life, and Blanchett has always tried to protect her children from media intrusion, limiting public family appearances and carefully choosing when and how to talk about her personal life. This decision to keep the family shielded from notoriety reflects a clear vision of her responsibility as a mother and wife, a desire to create a safe and normal space for her children, despite the extraordinary nature of her work.

Blanchett has often spoken of the challenge of balancing family life with such a demanding career. Despite being one of the most in-demand actresses in the world, she has always tried to make work decisions that allow her to reconcile her role as a mother with her role as an actress. On many occasions, she chose projects that allowed her to work close to home or that provided for shooting times compatible with family management. For example, during her directorship of the Sydney Theatre Company with Upton, the couple decided to live in Sydney with their children in order to provide them with as normal a life as possible. Blanchett has spoken several times about choosing to prioritise her family, despite the many career opportunities that would often take her away from home for long periods. This decision to find a balance between personal and professional life has defined many of her career choices, demonstrating her strong sense of responsibility as a mother and partner.

Being a mother has also influenced her perspective on her career and the social issues she has chosen to support. Blanchett explained that being a mother has given her a new awareness of future issues, particularly environmental ones. This new perspective has led her to become even more involved in environmental causes, recognising that decisions made today will directly affect future generations, including her children. Motherhood has added a dimension of responsibility to her choices, both in terms of social and professional engagement, making her actions even more conscious and focused. Blanchett also spoke about the joy and challenges of being a mother, emphasising how each child represents a continuous source of learning and personal growth, and how their love and presence are an anchor for her in a world that can sometimes seem unstable and overwhelming.

Despite her worldwide fame, Cate Blanchett has managed to keep a discreet profile when it comes to her private life. She rarely gets involved in scandals or gossip, and prefers to let her artistic achievements speak for her. Her reserve has become a hallmark of her public persona, reinforcing the idea that it is possible to maintain a high-profile career without sacrificing personal integrity. Blanchett has always tried to avoid the spotlight when it comes to her family, focusing instead on protecting their privacy and providing a safe and secure environment for her children. This choice of discretion has helped to make her one of the most respected figures on the film scene, a woman who has managed to maintain a balance between a brilliant career and a solid private life away from the spotlight.

The choice to maintain a discreet private life is also reflected in the rarity of her public appearances outside the professional context. Blanchett rarely attends social events and prefers to devote her free time to her family and the social and environmental commitments close to her heart. This distance from Hollywood glamour, despite being one of the most influential and award-winning actresses of her generation, has helped to reinforce Blanchett's perception as an authentic and centred person who is not distracted by the ephemeral. Her life with Andrew Upton and their children has remained anchored in values of respect, privacy and responsibility, and this approach has allowed Blanchett to maintain personal stability even in the context of a career that has taken her to the top of the film industry.

Cate Blanchett has managed to build an extraordinarily successful career without ever compromising her personal values or family life. Her bond with Andrew Upton, their mutual commitment to raising their children and the desire to maintain a balance between professional and private life have defined her existence off screen. Her love for her family and desire to protect their privacy have always taken precedence, and this has helped cement Cate's image not only as a talented actress, but also as a woman of great integrity and wisdom. Her approach to private life, characterised by discretion and respect, is a model for many celebrities trying to balance notoriety with family life, proving that it is possible to maintain a strong sense of personal identity even in the highly visible world of Hollywood.

Chapter 16. Collaboration with great filmmakers

Cate Blanchett's collaboration with some of the greatest directors in film history has played a crucial role in her career development and artistic growth. Working with visionaries such as Martin Scorsese, Todd Haynes and Peter Jackson has allowed Blanchett to engage with different styles and approaches, enriching her professional baggage and profoundly influencing her understanding of acting. Each of these directors brought a different nuance to her career, stimulating her to explore new sides of characters and to push the boundaries of traditional performance. These collaborations, though heterogeneous in genre and narrative, have all contributed to building Blanchett's image as a versatile actress, capable of adapting to any role with extraordinary depth and dedication.

One of Blanchett's first significant encounters with a major director was with Martin Scorsese in the film 'The Aviator' (2004), where she played the role of Katharine Hepburn, the legendary Hollywood actress. Scorsese, known for his meticulousness and rigorous approach to direction, pushed Blanchett to an unprecedented level of detail. Playing an iconic figure like Hepburn required not only a perfect understanding of the historical character, but also the ability to make her human and accessible.

Scorsese, with his passion for historical reconstruction and his love of detail, guided Blanchett through a process of total transformation, helping her capture every nuance of Hepburn's personality, from her eccentricities to her inner strength. This role marked a turning point in Blanchett's career, not only because it earned her her first Oscar for Best Supporting Actress, but also because it demonstrated her ability to play real, iconic characters with a sensitivity and intensity rarely seen on screen. Scorsese's influence on Blanchett was evident not only in her maniacal attention to detail, but also in the way she approached acting as a process of total immersion in character, a lesson the actress carried with her into many of her subsequent projects.

Her collaboration with Todd Haynes, a director known for his visually rich style and intimate stories, took Blanchett down a different, more experimental and psychological path. She worked with Haynes on two seminal films: 'I'm Not There' (2007) and 'Carol' (2015). In 'I'm Not There', Blanchett took on one of the most original challenges of her career, playing one of the six faces of Bob Dylan in a film that challenged narrative conventions and played with the concept of fluid identity. The role of Dylan, a male figure, was an exercise in radical transformation for Blanchett, allowing her to explore new ways of interpreting gender and personality on screen. Haynes, with his experimental approach, gave Blanchett the freedom to play with audience expectations, allowing her to reinvent herself as a performer and break the barriers of traditional character portrayal. In 'Carol', however, Haynes took Blanchett into more delicate and intimate territory, directing her in a forbidden love story between two women in the 1950s. Blanchett's performance was praised for its elegance and emotional depth, and working with Haynes allowed the actress to explore her character's vulnerability and passion in a story of social repression and personal discovery. Haynes's ability to create complex emotional worlds through poetic imagery and visually refined storytelling has influenced the way Blanchett has approached more nuanced and psychologically intense roles, pushing her to always seek emotional truth in her characters.

Her experience with Peter Jackson, director of the Lord of the Rings trilogy, represented another important milestone in Blanchett's career, allowing her to explore a completely different genre: epic fantasy. Playing Galadriel, the elven queen, Blanchett had the opportunity to work in a setting characterised by large-scale special effects, spectacular sets and a rich and complex mythology. Jackson, known for his grandiose cinematic vision and talent for handling epic narratives, was able to guide Blanchett in a role that required a commanding stage presence, but at the same time an inner delicacy. Galadriel, although a supernatural character, was played by Blanchett with a human depth that added a new dimension to the film. Working with Jackson allowed Blanchett to develop the ability to adapt to roles requiring not only acting skills but also constant interaction with technology and visual effects, a challenge that helped her expand her skills as an actress in a highly technical context.

Every director Blanchett has worked with has had a significant impact on her career, and in turn, the actress has influenced their work with her extraordinary ability to fully immerse herself in the characters. With Scorsese she learned the importance of attention to detail and historical accuracy, with Haynes she explored new psychological and narrative horizons, while with Jackson she broadened her experience in an epic genre that requires a monumental stage presence. These experiences have helped define her artistic vision, making her one of the most versatile and appreciated actresses of her generation. Blanchett's ability to adapt to a wide range of directing styles has made it possible for her to play different roles, always maintaining a consistency in the quality of her performances. The mutual impact between Blanchett and these directors has created some of the most memorable collaborations in film history, leading to the creation of films that have been not only critical and commercial successes, but also milestones in contemporary cinema.

Working with directors of such calibre has also influenced Blanchett's future choices, prompting her to constantly seek out projects that challenge her both artistically and technically. Her willingness to collaborate with extremely talented filmmakers has meant that each of her films has been an opportunity to grow as an artist and to explore new facets of acting. The respect and esteem that directors such as Scorsese, Haynes and Jackson have for Blanchett is a result of her tireless commitment and her extraordinary ability to bring complex and fascinating characters to the screen. This continuous pursuit of excellence has made Cate Blanchett one of the most respected and sought-after actresses in the world of cinema, an artist capable of leaving an indelible mark on every project in which she participates, thanks to her dedication, intelligence and extraordinary talent.

Chapter 17. Cate Blanchett and TV series

Cate Blanchett's decision to enter the world of TV series marked an important turning point in her career, confirming her ability to adapt to new formats and languages, without ever losing the depth and intensity that characterise her film interpretations. Although she was already recognised as one of the most talented actresses in contemporary cinema, her choice to work in television showed a willingness to explore a medium that has experienced a creative renaissance in recent years, becoming a space for experimentation and complex storytelling. Her entry into the world of TV series was marked by the great success of 'Mrs. America' (2020), a miniseries that was widely acclaimed by critics and audiences, and that allowed Blanchett to try her hand at a role of extraordinary complexity and historical relevance.

In 'Mrs. America', Blanchett plays Phyllis Schlafly, a central figure in the conservative movement of the 1970s who strongly opposed the Equal Rights Amendment, an amendment proposed in the United States to guarantee equal rights regardless of gender. The character of Schlafly was a challenge for Blanchett not only because she embodied a real and politically controversial woman, but also because the series presented a multifaceted portrait of an era of great social and cultural change.

Her performance managed to avoid any stereotypes, managing to convey the psychological and ideological complexity of a woman who fought to preserve an idea of society that may seem outdated today, but which garnered great support at the time. Blanchett brought to the stage a character full of contradictions: strong, cunning and charismatic, but at the same time a victim of a patriarchal system she sought to protect. Her performance was acclaimed for its ability to humanise a figure often painted in a two-dimensional way, allowing the audience to understand not only her motivations, but also the personal tensions that ran through her private and public life.

The success of 'Mrs. America' confirmed that Blanchett's choice to enter the world of TV series was not just a simple foray, but a project deeply connected to her quest for committed and challenging roles. Television, particularly limited series, offers actors the opportunity to explore characters more extensively than film. The narratives stretched over several episodes allow a psychological depth that films often cannot provide due to time constraints. This format allowed Blanchett to investigate every nuance of Schlafly's character, from her family life and personal insecurities to her relentless political determination. The series also provided an important historical context, dealing with issues such as feminism, civil rights and American politics, topics that are still reflected in contemporary society today. Blanchett, who has always been interested in projects with social and cultural relevance, found in 'Mrs. America' a perfect platform to combine her talent with political and social engagement, bringing to light one of the most controversial figures in 20th century American history.

One of the most interesting aspects of this choice is how Blanchett was able to navigate naturally between film and television, two worlds that, despite their differences, are becoming increasingly interconnected. The main difference between cinema and TV lies in the duration and nature of the storytelling. Whereas cinema often focuses on condensed stories, designed to be experienced in a single sitting, television allows for a more layered narrative, which evolves slowly and offers actors the chance to develop their characters more gradually. Blanchett has made the most of this opportunity, adapting to the different pace of the small screen without ever sacrificing the quality of her performance. Her ability to switch from one medium to another demonstrates her versatility and deep understanding of the demands of each format, allowing her to shine in both a two-hour film and a nine-episode series.

The impact of 'Mrs. America' on Cate Blanchett's TV career has opened up new perspectives, not only for her, but for many other high-calibre actresses who have found TV a fertile ground for complex and profound roles. Blanchett, who has always chosen her projects with care, has shown that she is able to recognise the potential of the small screen, not seeing it as a fallback, but as a new form of expression that allows her to further expand her repertoire. The success of the series has confirmed that TV can offer the same narrative quality as film, if not more, when supported by intelligent scripts and high-calibre production teams. This marks a significant change in the industry, where the barriers between film and television are gradually breaking down, and internationally renowned actors like Blanchett can switch between mediums without compromising their careers or status.

As for Cate Blanchett's future on the small screen, it is likely that she will continue to explore this format, given her success and the general appreciation of her performance in 'Mrs. America'. By selecting projects that address relevant and topical issues, Blanchett has shown that she has a strong instinct for stories that deserve to be told, and television, with its ability to reach a large and diverse audience, could become an increasingly important space for her. With the rise of streaming platforms and the increasing demand for quality content, TV offers endless possibilities for an actress of her calibre, and it is not hard to imagine that Blanchett will continue to seek out roles that allow her to challenge herself and explore characters rich in emotional and psychological complexity.

Cate Blanchett's decision to embrace the world of TV series with 'Mrs. America' was a pivotal moment in her career, proving that her search for meaningful and profound roles is not limited to the big screen. Television, with its long and multifaceted narratives, provided Blanchett with a new platform on which to shine, and the success of this TV foray paved the way for further opportunities in the future. With her ability to adapt to different formats and bring the same emotional intensity to each project, Blanchett has once again proven herself to be one of the most versatile and talented actresses of her generation, capable of excelling in both film and TV, leaving an indelible imprint in both worlds.

Chapter 18. Professional challenges

Throughout her career, Cate Blanchett has faced several professional challenges that have tested not only her versatility as an actress, but also her ability to make difficult decisions in an ever-changing industry. From the beginning, Blanchett chose to build a career based on complex and often controversial roles, avoiding the easier paths that could have guaranteed her immediate and commercial success. This inclination towards challenging roles pushed her to make courageous decisions, even when it meant risking mixed reactions from critics and audiences. One of the first challenges she faced was playing historical and royal figures, as in the case of 'Elizabeth' (1998), where she played Queen Elizabeth I. This role was loaded with expectations, not only because of the historical weight of the character, but also because several other actors had already played the sovereign in the past. Blanchett, however, was able to distinguish herself, bringing a new complexity to the role, embodying a woman who is powerful but vulnerable, decisive but also aware of her own frailties. Her performance, while almost universally praised, drew some criticism questioning her ability to play such an influential historical figure in a film era dominated by established actresses. However, instead of letting the criticism hold her back, Blanchett used this experience as a springboard to prove her worth, and her performance has become one of the most iconic of her career.

Another of the great challenges she had to face was the choice of controversial roles, characters that were not always easy to like or understand, requiring considerable emotional and psychological involvement. An emblematic example was her role in 'Blue Jasmine' (2013), directed by Woody Allen. The character of Jasmine is a disgraced, mentally unstable woman whose emotional breakdown is at the centre of the film. Playing such a disturbed character, who is in a constant state of psychological disorientation, required a special delicacy to avoid the risk of stereotyping her. Blanchett rose to the challenge with a performance that touched extraordinary levels of emotional intensity, but the role was not without controversy. Besides the difficult character, Blanchett also had to deal with the context of the accusations against Woody Allen, which cast a shadow over much of his work. Despite the heated debate surrounding the film, Blanchett handled the situation with great professionalism, distinguishing her work as an actress from outside controversy, and her performance was rewarded with an Oscar for Best Actress in a Leading Role. This was a significant moment in her career, in which she was able to prove that, even in the most complex contexts, she can bring performances of the highest level to the screen.

The difficult choices did not stop there. Blanchett has often accepted roles that other actresses might have avoided for fear of being relegated to a certain kind of stereotype or facing too heavy criticism. Another emblematic example was the film 'I'm Not There' (2007), directed by Todd Haynes, in which she played one of Bob Dylan's incarnations. Playing a music legend like Dylan, moreover as a woman playing a male role, was an unprecedented challenge. The risk of failure was very high, but Blanchett accepted the role with enthusiasm, demonstrating once again her ability to embrace complex roles and go beyond the limits of traditional acting. Her performance was praised by critics for its audacity and originality, and confirmed that Blanchett is an actress who is prepared to take artistic risks in order to always push beyond conventions. It is precisely this tendency to choose unconventional roles, characters that challenge expectations, that has allowed Blanchett to keep her career fresh and innovative, avoiding the danger of becoming trapped in one type of role.

Critics have not always been unanimous in their assessment of her choices. There have been times when some of her films have not been as successful as hoped or have been received coldly. However, Blanchett has shown that she has been able to cope with these difficulties with great resilience, without letting moments of crisis discourage her. Rather than avoiding risky projects, she continued to seek out roles that would challenge her, as in the case of her work in the theatre, where she experimented with equally challenging and profound roles, often in less secure and remunerative artistic contexts than in Hollywood. This approach proved that, despite the difficulties, her passion for acting and her desire to explore new artistic territories never failed.

Blanchett has been able to overcome the difficulties of her career through a combination of discipline, self-criticism and open-mindedness. Each challenge has been met with the awareness that growing professionally also means learning from failure or criticism. One of the aspects that has always characterised his path is his ability to constantly reinvent himself, avoiding repeating the same roles or falling into the trap of security. This determination to keep her career dynamic and challenging has led her to explore a wide range of genres and characters, from the epic 'Lord of the Rings' to the psychological drama 'Carol'. Her encounters with intellectually stimulating directors such as Peter Jackson, Todd Haynes and Martin Scorsese have been a key element in her artistic growth, but Blanchett has also always maintained a strong sense of independence, carefully choosing which projects to undertake and refusing to be defined by a single success or failure.

Blanchett has always preferred to tackle the most complex roles and greatest challenges, convinced that only through risk can one truly grow. Her ability to overcome difficulties with grace and determination has ensured that her career has continued to evolve and flourish, maintaining the interest of audiences and critics alike, and confirming her as one of the most influential figures on the international film scene.

Chapter 19. Female leadership in Hollywood

Cate Blanchett has played a key role in promoting female leadership in Hollywood, becoming not only a model of talent and dedication, but also a powerful voice for gender equality in the film industry. Throughout her career, Blanchett has demonstrated an extraordinary ability to use her influence and visibility to address issues of great social relevance, particularly those related to women's rights and gender inequality in the film industry. Her commitment to equality has manifested itself in numerous ways, both through her work on screen and behind the scenes, and her constant promotion of female partnerships has helped create a new awareness of the importance of representation and equity in the entertainment industry.

One of the most noticeable aspects of Cate Blanchett's leadership role has been her commitment to playing strong, complex female characters that challenge traditional gender stereotypes. Through her choice of roles that highlight independent, powerful and multidimensional women, Blanchett has helped redefine the way women are portrayed on the silver screen. In films such as 'Carol', 'Blue Jasmine' and 'Elizabeth', she has brought to light female figures who are not merely sidekicks or supporting characters, but are central protagonists of their stories. This approach inspired numerous other

95

actresses to seek similar roles, and helped push directors and screenwriters to write scripts that offered wider opportunities for women. Blanchett, through her example, demonstrated that commercial success does not have to come from conventional roles, but can also be achieved through the exploration of characters that face complex personal and social challenges.

Her role as a role model for women in Hollywood was also reflected in her public activism, where she took a stand on crucial issues such as unequal pay and lack of opportunities for female directors and producers. Blanchett was one of the leading voices in the #MeToo movement, which lifted the veil on the widespread abuse of power and sexual harassment in the film industry. During the film awards, she has never hesitated to speak openly about the need for greater gender equality and the need to reform the entire industry structure to ensure women have the same career opportunities as men. In particular, in her speech at the Oscars in 2014, when she won Best Actress in a Leading Role for 'Blue Jasmine', Blanchett emphasised the importance of recognising women's stories, stating that films about women are not a 'niche genre', but have universal and commercial value. These kinds of statements helped change the public discourse on gender equality in Hollywood, proving that stories led by female protagonists can be, and often are, box office successes.

Cate Blanchett's activism has also had a tangible impact behind the scenes, through promoting collaborations with other women in the film industry. During her time as co-artistic director of the Sydney Theatre Company with her husband Andrew Upton, Blanchett strongly supported the involvement of female directors, writers and producers in the company's theatre and film projects. This inclusive approach has allowed many women to emerge in an industry historically dominated by men, and has paved the way for greater diversity and representation behind the scenes. Blanchett has always recognised the importance of collective work and has often emphasised that successful productions are the result of collaborative teams that include diverse voices and multiple perspectives. Her insistence on creating opportunities for women, not only in front of the camera but also behind it, has had a profound impact on the industry, contributing to a slow but steady evolution towards greater inclusion.

Another significant aspect of her commitment to gender equality has been her involvement in projects that put social and political issues related to women's rights at the centre of narratives. With 'Mrs. America' (2020), a television series chronicling the movement to ratify the Equal Rights Amendment in the United States and the opposition to it, Blanchett played the role of Phyllis Schlafly, a conservative figure who opposed the amendment.

Although Schlafly was a character ideologically distant from Blanchett's positions, the actress chose this role for its complexity and the opportunity to explore political dynamics that still have a great impact on women's lives today. 'Mrs. America' was a perfect example of how Blanchett uses her work not only as a vehicle for entertainment, but also as a platform to raise awareness of crucial issues. Her choice to engage in projects that touch on important social issues reflects her desire to use her visibility to promote greater awareness and change.

Cate Blanchett's female leadership in Hollywood also manifests itself in her commitment to creating a more equitable and sustainable industry. Blanchett has often emphasised the importance of structures that ensure gender equality not only in creative decisions, but also in the economic and organisational management of film and theatre productions. She has advocated the adoption of policies that promote equal pay for men and women in the film industry, an issue on which she has spoken publicly on several occasions. In addition, her commitment to sustainability ties in with her vision of a film world that not only promotes gender equality, but is also committed to reducing its environmental impact, in line with her struggles for climate justice.

Cate Blanchett represents a model of female leadership that goes beyond mere personal success, extending to the desire to create systemic change in the film industry. Her ability to combine an extraordinary career with a concrete commitment to gender equality and social justice distinguishes her as one of the most influential and respected figures in the entertainment industry. Her career choices and activism helped strengthen the women's rights movement in Hollywood and inspired an entire generation of actresses, directors and industry professionals to demand a more equal and inclusive space. Blanchett has shown that the power of a successful career can and should be used to build a fairer industry, where women's voices are heard and valued, and where talent and merit are not determined by gender. Her efforts will continue to leave a lasting mark, positively influencing the future of Hollywood and opening new avenues for women in film and theatre.

Chapter 20. The evolution of her acting style

The evolution of Cate Blanchett's acting style has been an ongoing process, a transformation that has spanned the various stages of her career and has seen the actress grow, mature and adapt to increasingly complex and multifaceted roles. From the very beginning, Blanchett has shown remarkable versatility, a quality that has become the hallmark of her craft. However, her approach to acting has evolved gradually, allowing her to refine her techniques and bring ever deeper interpretations to the screen. One of the most interesting aspects of Blanchett's artistic journey is her ability to constantly explore new territories and never settle for success. Each new role represents a challenge and an opportunity for her to grow, and this relentless quest for improvement has profoundly marked her acting style. If in her early career Blanchett tended to build her characters with a more instinctive approach, over time she has developed a greater awareness of the inner processes that animate her protagonists, deepening her understanding of the psychological dynamics that govern them.

One of the moments that marked a significant turning point in her career was her portrayal of Elizabeth I in the 1998 film 'Elizabeth'. In this role, Blanchett displayed her ability to blend emotional power and formal control, a combination that characterised many of her later performances. Her Elizabeth is both vulnerable and authoritarian, a young woman who must quickly adapt to power in a male-dominated world. This role required Blanchett to measure herself against the history and iconography of a real character, a task that demanded a high degree of preparation and discipline. The experience in 'Elizabeth' consolidated her reputation and prompted her to explore roles of other historical figures, such as Katharine Hepburn in Martin Scorsese's 'The Aviator', where she further honed her ability to embody real-life characters, balancing fidelity to reality and personal interpretation.

Over the years, her acting style began to reflect an artistic maturity that made her performances increasingly subtle and layered. In her most recent roles, such as in Woody Allen's 'Blue Jasmine', Blanchett has shown a mastery of acting that transcends mere technique to an emotional depth that touches the audience's most intimate chords. In 'Blue Jasmine', her portrayal of a woman on the verge of emotional and psychological breakdown is a perfect example of how Blanchett is able to delve into the souls of her characters, showing all their fragilities and the contradictions that inhabit them. This role required a particular subtlety: Jasmine is a complex character, alternating between moments of lucidity and states of mental confusion, and Blanchett managed to maintain this balance with a mastery that earned her a well-deserved Oscar. Here, her acting style appears completely evolved, characterised by a capacity for total identification that has never lost sight of the character's humanity, even in her most difficult moments.

Another key aspect of the evolution of her style has been her ability to seamlessly switch between commercial and art-house cinema. Blanchett has worked with some of the world's most influential directors, adapting to very different artistic visions. Directors such as Peter Jackson, Todd Haynes and Terrence Malick have helped shape her career, influencing the way she approaches characters and enriching her acting with new nuances. In particular, the experience of working with Todd Haynes on films such as 'Carol' and 'I'm Not There' was decisive for his artistic development. Haynes, known for his attention to detail and visually evocative narratives, pushed Blanchett to explore new modes of expression, leading her to play roles charged with emotional and symbolic intensity. In 'Carol', her portrayal of a woman experiencing a forbidden love affair in the 1950s was praised for its elegance and ability to convey deep emotions with minimalist, controlled acting. This contrast between control and passion has become one of Blanchett's stylistic hallmarks, a balance that allows her to tackle very different roles without ever being repetitive.

The evolution of her acting style is also reflected in her ability to experiment with extremely different roles, as demonstrated by her work in blockbusters, where she has been able to bring the same intensity and seriousness that characterises her approach to smaller films. In 'Thor: Ragnarok' (2017), where she plays Hela, the goddess of death, Blanchett proved that she is able to dominate the screen even in a purely entertaining context, giving her character an imposing and charismatic stage presence. Her portrayal of Hela is an example of how, while moving within a fantasy and spectacular genre, Blanchett still manages to infuse a character with depth and complexity, making her memorable. This ability to adapt to all kinds of roles, without ever losing her artistic identity, is one of the elements that define her evolution as an actress.

Throughout her career, Blanchett has often reflected on her artistic maturity and how her approach to acting has changed over time. If as a young actress she often let her instincts guide her, today she is much more aware of the emotional and psychological mechanisms that come into play during a performance. This does not mean that she has lost the freshness of her early performances, but rather that she has developed a greater mastery of her talent, knowing when to let go and when to maintain total control over the scene. This awareness of her art has allowed her to tackle increasingly complex roles, in which the psychology of the characters is at the centre of the narrative, as in 'Manifesto' (2015), an experimental film in which Blanchett plays thirteen different characters, each with her own personality and cultural background. This project represented a real artistic challenge, and highlighted her ability to adapt to radically different acting styles within the same film.

The evolution of Cate Blanchett's acting style is the result of a constant process of learning, experimentation and reflection. Her career has been marked by a constant search for roles that challenge her and allow her to grow both as an actress and as a person. Each experience, each film, each collaboration with talented directors has contributed to the emergence of new nuances in her acting, making her one of the most complete and appreciated performers on the contemporary film scene. Her artistic maturity is not only the result of years of experience, but also of a constant intellectual curiosity and a deep passion for her craft, which continues to guide her towards new challenges and goals.

Chapter 21. International awards and accolades

Throughout her extraordinary career, Cate Blanchett has collected an impressive number of international awards and accolades, reflecting not only her versatility and talent as an actress, but also the profound impact she has had on the global film industry. Among the most prestigious honours she has received are two Oscars, three Golden Globes, three BAFTAs, and numerous other awards that testify to the consistent excellence of her work. Her first Oscar came in 2005 for her portrayal of Katharine Hepburn in Martin Scorsese's film 'The Aviator', where she masterfully embodied the energy and complexity of one of Hollywood's greatest icons. This role, which won her the Oscar for Best Supporting Actress, was a sign of how Blanchett was capable of dominating the international scene, bringing to the cinema a performance full of detail and sensitivity. Her win was not only a recognition of her acting talent, but also a celebration of her ability to completely transform herself into each character she plays, with a fidelity to historical and psychological details that won over critics and audiences alike.

Her second Oscar, won in 2014 as Best Actress in a Leading Role for Woody Allen's Blue Jasmine, further confirmed her status as one of the most talented and respected actresses on the contemporary film scene. Her portrayal of Jasmine, a woman facing a psychological breakdown after losing everything, was praised for its emotional intensity and the complexity with which Blanchett was able to make her character's suffering human and authentic. Here, the award emphasised how her career was now established at the highest level and how she was able to tackle difficult and controversial roles with extraordinary naturalness and grace. The Oscar for 'Blue Jasmine' had a significant impact on her career, as it showed that Blanchett was not only capable of establishing herself in independent productions and more intimate projects, but that she could also single-handedly carry the weight of an entire film, attracting critical attention and winning over audiences with her emotionally complex performance.

In addition to the Oscars, Blanchett has won numerous Golden Globes, awards that have further consolidated her international reputation. She won her first Golden Globe for 'Elizabeth' in 1999, an award that marked the beginning of her rise in the film world. This iconic role showcased her ability to play historical figures with depth and charisma, and her Golden Globe win was an important consecration of her career, allowing her to be considered one of the most promising actresses of her generation. Subsequently, she won other Golden Globes for films such as 'I'm Not There' and 'Blue Jasmine', demonstrating a continuity in her artistic excellence and confirming her status as a reference actress in every film genre.

Even the BAFTAs, the prestigious British film awards, have recognised her talent several times. Blanchett won her first BAFTA for 'The Aviator' in 2005 and went on to receive awards from the British Academy for several performances, including 'Blue Jasmine'. Her constant presence at the BAFTAs is a testimony to the fact that her appeal is global, and that her talent is appreciated not only in Hollywood, but worldwide. International critics have consistently praised her ability to adapt to any role, bringing complex and often emotionally turbulent characters to the screen, but always with a grace and power that distinguish her as an uncommon performer.

The impact of these awards on her career has been indisputable. Each award helped cement her reputation as one of the best actresses of her time, allowing her to choose more and more interesting and challenging roles. The awards have also expanded her global visibility, making her an influential figure not only in film, but also in areas such as theatre and television, where she has continued to distinguish herself. However, Blanchett has always had a balanced view of awards, seeing them as a recognition of collective work rather than a definitive measure of success. In several interviews, she has expressed gratitude for the awards she has received, but has also emphasised that they are not the only yardstick for assessing an actor's worth. For Blanchett, the art of acting is first and foremost a creative process, a personal journey that is enriched with each new role, and awards, while gratifying, are not the sole focus of her work.

Her view of awards as a measure of success is also reflected in the way she has managed her career. Blanchett has never chosen her roles based on the possibility of winning an award, but has always followed her instincts, preferring projects that would stimulate her artistically and allow her to grow as an actress. Even after reaching the pinnacle of success with two Oscars and countless other awards, Blanchett has continued to explore roles in independent and experimental productions, demonstrating a dedication to her craft that goes beyond the simple desire to accumulate accolades. Her commitment to acting has always been linked to a deep passion for storytelling and discovering new aspects of the human condition, and this sincerity in her approach has helped make her one of the most respected and admired figures in the film world.

In light of all this, it is clear that awards and accolades have played an important role in defining Cate Blanchett's career, but they have never restricted her artistic freedom or influenced her choices in a decisive way. On the contrary, awards have been a confirmation for her of what she already knew: that her work is appreciated and that it has the power to touch the hearts and minds of audiences in a deep and lasting way. This combination of talent, dedication and humility is what has made Blanchett not only an award-winning actress of international renown, but also a model of professionalism and integrity in the film world. In the future, she is likely to continue to reap accolades for her work, but what is truly significant is the way she has been able to maintain a clear and consistent vision of her art, remaining true to herself and her principles, regardless of the number of trophies on her shelves.

Chapter 22. A legacy of class and talent

Cate Blanchett's legacy in the world of film and theatre is destined to endure as a symbol of class, talent and artistic dedication. Since her early days, Blanchett has embodied a model of acting excellence, pushing the boundaries of her craft and leaving a profound mark on all the works in which she has participated. Her ability to range between dramatic, historical, comic and even fantasy roles, without ever losing sight of the emotional and psychological complexity of the characters, has made her name synonymous with quality in an industry that often favours superficiality. Blanchett has been able to distinguish herself not only for her acting talent, but also for her artistic integrity, refusing to be limited by industry-imposed boundaries and always following her instincts when choosing roles. This combination of virtues has made her one of the most influential figures in contemporary cinema, inspiring entire generations of actors, directors and viewers, and charting a course that many other artists seek to follow.

One of the most significant aspects of Blanchett's legacy is her versatility. She has successfully played a wide range of characters, from powerful queens such as Elizabeth I, to contemporary women grappling with personal crises, such as Jasmine in 'Blue Jasmine', to legendary and supernatural figures such as Galadriel in the 'Lord of the Rings' trilogy. This ability to adapt to such diverse roles has allowed her to explore a wide range of emotions and themes, making each of her performances an opportunity to challenge herself and offer the audience something new and unexpected. Not only has she demonstrated an extraordinary capacity for physical and vocal metamorphosis, but she has also been able to bring an emotional and intellectual depth to each role, creating characters that remain etched in the collective memory. It is this thoughtful and searching approach that has defined his career and will continue to be remembered as an integral part of his contribution to cinema.

In addition to her impact in front of the camera, Cate Blanchett also left an indelible mark on the theatre, particularly with her work at the Sydney Theatre Company, where she served as co-artistic director for several years with her husband Andrew Upton. During her tenure, Blanchett brought a new vitality to the Australian theatre scene, introducing ambitious and experimental productions, and bringing Australian theatre to international attention. This commitment to theatre demonstrates how Blanchett is a well-rounded artist, able to move with equal ease between film and stage, always maintaining the highest standards of quality. Her theatre work has profoundly influenced not only the local but also the global art scene, proving that theatre can be a laboratory for innovation as much as film, and that performance art has the power to transform those who participate in it, both as artists and spectators.

Cate Blanchett's influence on future generations of actors and directors is evident. Her dedication to acting, her respect for artistry and her constant pursuit of roles that defy convention have inspired an entire generation of performers to not compromise, to always seek authenticity and depth in their performances. Many younger actresses see Blanchett as a role model, not only for her success, but for the way she has built a career based on quality and artistic integrity. Blanchett has shown that true success does not lie in fame or awards, but in the ability to stay true to oneself and continue to grow as an artist. Her ability to make courageous decisions, choosing roles that others might have avoided for fear of failure or judgement, has opened up new avenues for many artists, encouraging them to explore their creativity without fear.

Her place in film history is now unquestionable. Blanchett is one of the most awarded and respected actresses of her generation, with a career that spans decades and is studded with iconic performances. Her influence extends far beyond film; she is a leading figure in the gender equality debate in Hollywood, and has used her position to promote equality and sustainability, demonstrating that artists have a responsibility not only to their work, but also to society. Her leadership in the women's rights movement, her commitment to supporting social and environmental causes, and her ability to gracefully meet the challenges of her career have made her a symbol of class, strength and determination.

For audiences, Cate Blanchett is more than just an actress: she is a cultural icon. Every one of her screen appearances is eagerly anticipated, because she always brings something unique and authentic to each role. Her ability to connect with the viewer, to communicate deep emotions without ever coming across as artificial, is what makes her work so special. Blanchett has a rare ability to make even the most complex characters accessible, allowing the audience to identify with them, to understand them and to feel involved in their stories. This emotional connection she manages to create with the audience is one of the key elements of her artistic legacy, and is something that continues to inspire both audiences and artists who aspire to follow in her footsteps.

Her impact on the entertainment industry and popular culture is bound to endure. Cate Blanchett has proven that art is not just a matter of talent, but of dedication, intellectual curiosity and passion for the truth. She has turned each role into an acting lesson, showing that an actor's greatness lies not only in technical ability, but also in the ability to listen to and fully inhabit each character. Her legacy is that of an artist who balanced success and integrity, and helped redefine what it means to be an actress in an ever-changing industry. She will continue to inspire generations of artists by her example, proving that true greatness lies in always remaining open to growth and change, never losing sight of the importance of art as a tool for human connection and reflection on the world around us.

---Conclusion---

Having traced Cate Blanchett's extraordinary career, it is clear that her contribution to the world of film and theatre goes far beyond simply playing memorable roles. Blanchett has proven to be an artist who not only lives in the present, but also constantly looks to the future, helping to redefine the role of women in the film and theatre industry, and becoming a reference point for future generations. Her ability to span genres, to masterfully interpret complex and profound characters, and to bring to the screen and stage performances that touch the hearts and minds of audiences, has made her one of the most influential and respected actresses of her generation. But Cate Blanchett's legacy does not stop there. Her dedication to social and environmental causes, her leadership in the gender equality movement and her commitment to promoting inclusive and conscious art are equally part of her global impact. Blanchett has been able to turn every challenge into an opportunity for personal and professional growth, proving that true talent is not limited to acting ability, but is expressed in the continuous quest for improvement and the willingness to confront the most important issues of our time. Her influence extends far beyond the confines of cinema: she is a leading figure in the debate on gender inequality in Hollywood and has used her position of power to promote positive change within the industry. Her commitment to equality and justice has inspired many actresses, directors and industry professionals not to settle and to fight for an equal place in show business. Blanchett has shown that a successful career can and should be used to advance important battles, and that the power of art also lies in its ability to transform society.

As we look to the future of her career, it is clear that Cate Blanchett still has much to offer, not only as an actress, but also as a cultural leader. Her ability to continually evolve, accept new challenges and remain true to her principles makes her an extraordinary figure, capable of inspiring not only audiences, but also her colleagues and new generations of artists. Blanchett has already left an indelible mark on the history of cinema and theatre, but it is equally certain that she will continue to explore new territories, seek out roles that challenge and enrich her, and influence the way cinema and theatre address the most pressing contemporary issues.

Ultimately, Cate Blanchett is more than a great actress. She is a complete artist, a woman who has managed to combine talent, passion, commitment and intelligence in a career that is a model for all those who want to leave a lasting mark on the art world. Her legacy, built on years of tireless work, courageous choices and extraordinary performances, will continue to inspire and influence the entertainment world for many years to come. Blanchett has shown that art can be a vehicle for change, that an actor can have an impact beyond the silver screen, and that true success is measured not just in awards and accolades, but in the ability to transform one's craft into a powerful and meaningful form of expression capable of improving the world we live in.

Cate Blanchett: Icon of Style and Success

The official tribute to the contemporary film muse and award-winning world star

Daniela Connor Grayson

Made in the USA
Monee, IL
12 December 2024

73470140R00068